A man in a movie theater noticed what looked like a goat sitting next to him. "Are you a goat?" asked the man, surprised. "Yes", said the goat." What are you doing at the movies?" The goat replied, "Well, I liked the book!"

A giraffe walks into a job center. "Wow, a talking giraffe," says the clerk. "With your talent, I'm sure we can find you a gig in the circus." "The circus?" says the giraffe, disappointed: "What does a circus want with a lawyer?"

Two fools are in the outback. It's getting dark, so they want to light a fire. One fool says to the other, "Are you sure these matches work?" The other fool replies, "I'm 100% sure. I tried them all!"

A man runs into the office of a psychiatrist and says, "Doc, you have to help me! My wife thinks she's a chicken and I don't know what to do!" The psychiatrist, still somewhat shocked by the man bursting into his office, says, "OK, I see. Tell me, how long has she had this condition?" "One-and-a-half years," says the man. "That long, you say?!", the psychiatrist said, "Why didn't you come to see me earlier?" The man shrugs his shoulders and replies: "We needed the eggs."

Q: What is orange and really bad for your teeth?
A: A brick!

Q: What's a shark's favorite lunch dish?
A: Peanut butter and jellyfish sandwich!

A young boy came home from school with a black eye. "What happened?", his mother asked "I had a big fight with my classmate," the boy replied, "He called me a sissy." "And, what did you do?", the mother asked. The little boy said, "I hit him with my purse!"

Q: On which Spanish island do they eat pizza every single day?
A: Ipizza!

Q: What do you call an alligator wearing a blue vest?
A: An investigator!

Q: Why is six so scared of seven?
A: Because seven "ate" nine!

Q: Why did the blonde woman run around her bed?
A: Because she was trying to catch up on her sleep!

Two buffalos are sitting on opposite sides of a river. One buffalo yells to the other, "How do I get to the other side of the river?" To which the other buffalo replies, "You ARE on the other side!"

Two fools are waiting at a traffic light. Then, one fool says,""It's green", to which the other fool replies, "Ehm, let me see...is it a cucumber?"

Q: How did the frog die?
A: He Kermit suicide...

Q: Of all the pets, which one makes the most noise?
A: A trumpet!

"It's not fair!", Sallie says to her mother. "What isn't fair, sweetie?", her mom replies. Sallie says, "You are married to dad, grandma is married to grandpa, but I have to marry a complete stranger!"

A mouse and an elephant are walking in the desert, in the scorching hot sun. After a while, the elephant starts to complain about the heat, "I'm being roasted alive!". The mouse replies, "Well, you can walk in MY shade for the next hour, if you want!"

Three man are sitting in a bar. The first man says: "After reading the book 'The Two Sisters', my daughter had twins." Then, the second man says: "Wow, same story here: my wife had triplets after reading 'The Three Musketeers'!" All of a sudden, the third man jumps off his chair, slams money on the table to pay for his drinks and grabs his jacket. "Where are you going?", the men ask. To which the third man replies, "My wife is reading 'The Hundred and One Dalmatians' RIGHT NOW!"

Knock, Knock.
Who's there?
Hatch.
Hatch who?
Bless you!

A ghost is waiting in line at the supermarket when he sees another ghost, waiting in the other line. Concerned, he asks: "Caspar, are you OK? You look a little pale..."

Q: Why did the marathon runner stop listening to music during his runs?
A: Because he broke too many records!

After not seeing one another for a couple of years, two old friends bump into each other at a basketball game. Matthew: "What's up, bro, how are you doing these days?" Rob: "I'm a PHD." Jerry: "Wow! That's crazy, you're a doctor, now?!"
Rob: "No, Pizza Home Delivery."

One day, a man was walking in a shopping mall when he noticed a sign in a store window that said "Help Wanted." The man didn't waste a second, ran in the store and yelled out, "What's wrong?"

Nurse: "Doctor, the invisible man just arrived for his 4pm appointment with you." Doctor: "Please tell him I'm sorry, I can't see him right now."

A fool walks into the room and says, "Doctor, lately I've been having trouble with my eyesight". The man in front of him replies, "You're very right, my good man. This is a Mexican restaurant!"

A man is walking along a beach in California when he finds a bottle. He picks it up and rubs it. All of a sudden, a genie appears and says, "Hello stranger, this is your lucky day. I will grant you one wish!" "Wow, this is my lucky day indeed," says the man, "My mom lives in Hawaii, and I never liked flying that much. Could you make a highway from Los Angeles all the way to Hawaii?"

The genie replies, "Do you know how much of my power that would take?" The man says, "Okay, okay, let me change my wish. I have had a lot of bad luck dating girls. Can you help me find a girl to date?" The genie responds, "So, that highway: do you want that with two lanes or four lanes?

A man takes his golden retriever to the vet, because he is cross-eyed. The vet says, "Let's have a look" and picks up the dog to examine his eyes. After looking at his eyes for a while, the vet says, "I'm going to have to put him down." "Wait, what?", the man replies, "Just because he is cross-eyed?" The vet says, "No, because he is really heavy!"

A science teacher wants to test if his students remember what he told them yesterday. Teacher: "Class, can anyone tell me what the chemical formula for water is?"
George: "HIJKLMNO."
Teacher: "George, what on earth are you talking about?"
George: "Yesterday, you told us it is H to O!"

Shaun walked into the doctor's office for a health check-up. "I have some good news and some bad news," the doctor said. "I'll start with the good news: you only have 24 hours left to live." "That's the good news?!", Shaun replied, with panic in his eyes. "Yes," the doctor responded, "The bad news is that I should have told you this yesterday."

Q: If you were to cross a dog and a calculator, what would you get?
A: A friend you can count on!

Q: What did the big chimney say to the little chimney?
A: "Sorry kid, you're too young to smoke."

Knock, Knock
Who's there?
Boo.
Boo who?
Please don't cry. It's only a joke!

Two brothers, John and Trouble, are playing hide and seek. John hides behind a police car. When a police officer sees John, he says: "Hey little boy, you're not allowed to sit here." To which John replies, "I can't leave, or else I'll be seen!" The officer gets angry and says, "Are you looking for trouble, boy?". To which John responds, "No officer, Trouble is looking for me!"

One day, a llama walks into a shop and asks the clerk if they sell walnuts. The clerk says, "No, we don't sell walnuts." The llama goes home and returns the next day, "Hello, do you sell walnuts?" Again, the clerk says they don't. The llama leaves the shop but returns the very next day. "There he is again," says the clerk to himself. And sure enough, the llama asks the clerk if they sell walnuts.

This time though, the clerk is so fed up with this stupid llama that he says, "No, llama, we don't sell walnuts! And if you come back one more time and ask me this question again, I will nail your feet to the floor!" The llama looks shocked and leaves the shop.

But...the clerk can't believe his eyes when he sees the llama walk through the door AGAIN, the next day. This time, the llama asks, "Do you have any nails?" The clerk says, "No, we don't have any nails." "Okay, good," the llama says, "Do you sell walnuts?"

Q: If a plane crashed on the border of the U.S. and Mexico, in which country would the survivors be buried?
A: In none of the two: you don't bury survivors!

Q: What do chickens serve to their friends at birthday parties?
A: Coop-cakes!

Two grains of sand are crossing the desert. All of sudden, one grain of sand says to the other: "Don't move, be very still...we're surrounded!"

Mom walks in the living room and finds her son Billy crying. After she learned what had happened, she turns to her other son and asks: "Joshua, why did you kick your brother in the stomach?" Joshua: "It was an accident...He turned around!"

One Saturday morning, a wife said to her husband: "Our dog is so smart. He brings in the daily newspapers every single morning!" Her husband responded: "Yes, he's a great dog, but lots of dogs can do that." "Yes, but we've never subscribed to any...", the wife replied.

George: "Why do alligators wear pink nail polish?" Rachel: "I don't have a clue." George: "To hide in cherry trees." Rachel: "Come on, George. I have never seen an alligator in a cherry tree." George: "See, it works!"

Teacher: "Is there anyone in this class who considers him- or herself stupid? If so, please stand up!" Everybody remains seated. Teacher: "Come on class, surely someone here must feel stupid, right?" Monica stands up. Teacher: "Oh, Monica, do you think you're stupid?" Monica: "No, teacher. I just feel bad that you're the only one standing!"

Q: Why is a vampire so easy to fool?
A: Because he is a sucker!

A man took his guinea pig to the vet. The doctor shook his head as he looked at the guinea pig. "I'm sorry, I'm afraid your guinea pig is dead", said the vet. "Wait, what, how could you be so sure?" the man replied.

So, the vet left the room and came back with a Labrador Retriever. The dog stood up on its hind legs, sniffed the guinea pig and shook its head. The vet left the room again. This time, he came back with a cat. The cat also sniffed the guinea pig and also shook its head. Then, the vet said that the guinea pig was now 100% dead.

With the man still in shock, the vet handed him the bill.

The man looked at the bill, in disbelief: "$750...why $750?!" The vet replied "If you had believed me when I first said it, it would have been $100. But you didn't believe me. So, to confirm the death, you also had a lab report and a cat scan!"

One day, a woman walks into a store to get some groceries. When she's done, she goes to the clerk to pay. The clerk looks at her items and sees 3 tomatoes, yogurt, a chocolate bar, and cheese. "Let me guess, you must be single," the clerk says. The woman, surprised, answers, "Well yes, how can you tell?" The clerk replies, "Because you're ugly."

Q: What's a dog's favorite kind of pizza?
A: Pupperoni!

I have this friend, and he thinks he is really smart. One day, he tried to convince me that an onion is the only food that can make you cry. So I grabbed a coconut and threw it at his face...

Knock, Knock!
Who is there?
Chicken.
Chicken who?
Chicken your pockets, maybe you'll find your keys there!

Q: Two toilet rolls are sitting in a bar. What did the first toilet roll say to the other?
A: "People keep on ripping me off!"

Teacher: "Class, who can tell me where the Declaration of Independence was signed?"
Jimmy: "At the bottom of the page!"

Q: What is even more amazing than a talking bear?
A: A spelling bee!

Q: What is light as a feather yet big as a house?
A: The shade of a house!

John: "Wow, I just fell off a 40 ft. ladder."
Hank: "Oh my, are you okay?"
John: "Yeah. It's a good thing I fell off the first step."

Two moms are talking about their sons, over a cup of tea.
Mother 1: "I really have the perfect son, you know?"
Mother 2: "Tell me, does he ever come home late?"
Mother 1: "No, never."
Mother 2: "Does he drink beer?"
Mother 1: "No, he never even had a glass of alcohol."
Mother 2: "Does he smoke?"
Mother 1: "No, he never lit a cigarette in his life!"
Mother 2: "Wow, I'm impressed! I guess you really do have the perfect son...How old is he?"
Mother 1: "He will be six months old next Friday."

Q: What do you call a dog magician?
A: A labracadabrador!

Q: How can you use water to create light?
A: By cleaning the windows!

Two fortune tellers bump into each other in the gym. Says one to the other, "You look better than next week!"

Q: If you have 15 oranges in one hand and 12 bananas in the other, what do you have?
A: Big hands!

Joshua: "Did you hear the news item about the kidnapping at school?"
Shane: "Yes, I saw it. You don't need to worry about it though. He just woke up."

Q: Can a kangaroo jump higher than the Statue of Liberty?
A: Of course! The Statue of Liberty can't jump, silly.

One day, a woman walked into a lawyer's office and said, "My colleague owes me $400 and she won't pay up. I'm here for legal advice; what should I do?" The lawyer thought about it for a few seconds, and then asked: "Do you have any proof you loaned her the money?". "Unfortunately, I don't," the woman replied. "OK, then here's what you should do. Write her an email asking her for the $4,000 she owes you," the lawyer said. "But she only owes me $400, though!" the woman replied. "Indeed. That's what she will reply. That email will be your proof!"

Q: Why did all the students in class eat their homework?
A: Because their teacher told them: "It's a piece of cake!"

Q: A boy volcano was located next to a girl volcano. What did he say to her?
A: "I lava you..."

Q: Why are the hairs of bees so sticky?
A: Because they use honey combs for it!

Q: Why do giraffes make terrible dance partners?
A: They've got two left feet!

Q: What do you get when you cross a Golden Retriever with a telephone?
A: A golden receiver!

Q: What happens to the car of a frog when it breaks down?
A: The car gets toad away!

Q: Why is it a bad idea to write a letter with a broken pencil?
A: Because it is pointless!

Q: Why is it a bad idea to tell a joke to an egg?
A: Because it might very well crack up!

Q: What did the left eye say to the right eye?
A: Between you and me, there is something that smells!

Q: What would you call a belt with a watch attached to it?
A: A waist of time!

Knock, Knock.
Who's there?
Lettuce.
Lettuce who?
Lettuce in. It's freezing outside!

Q: What did one hat say to the other hat?
A: Stay here, I'll go on a head!

A woman arrives at the train station and approaches the station master. Woman: "Excuse me, is this my train?" Station Master: "No, Mam, it belongs to the railway company." The woman, a bit taken aback: "That's funny, you got me there. However, what I meant to ask is if I can take this train to Chicago." Station Master: "No Mam, it's too heavy for that."

One day, a man visited his friend. When he walked into the living room, he found his friend playing chess with a lion. Astonished, he watched the game for a couple of minutes. "I can't believe my eyes!" he exclaimed. "That is the smartest lion I have ever seen." To which his friend replied: "Mwoah, he's not that smart. I've beaten him three games out of five..."

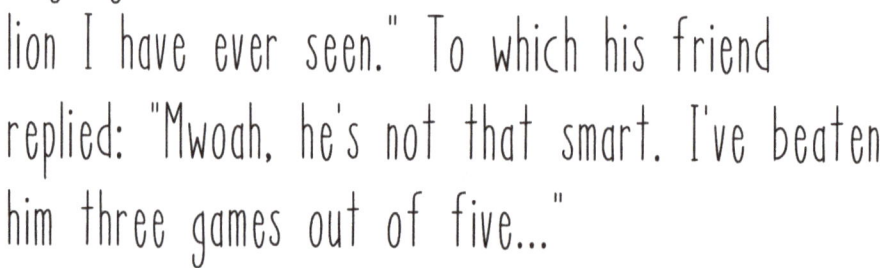

Q: What is a question that has a different answer each time you ask it?
A: 'What time is it?'

Q: How does one ocean say hello to another ocean?
A: He waves!

Q: What are a ninja's favorite kind of shoes?
A: Sneakers.

Q: What type of book has no story, but lots of characters?
A: A telephone book!

In the car on the way back from baseball practice, a little boy asks his father, "Dad, how do parents pick the names for their children?" "Well, my boy," his father responds, "The night before the mother is scheduled to give birth, the father goes into the forest with his tent and a few beers, to camp for the night. It is tradition that, when he wakes up the next morning, the first thing he sees when he leaves his tent is what he will name his child. That's why I named your brother Flying Eagle. What made you ask this question, Fox Poop?"

Q: What do you call the security men keeping guard outside a Samsung shop?
A: Guardians of the Galaxy!

Q: Why is Peter Pan always flying through the sky?
A: Because he Neverlands!

Q: Why did the fool throw his watch out of the window?
A: He wanted to see time fly!

Q: What type of nails do carpenters not like to hit?
A: Fingernails!

Q: Why does a pirate not know the alphabet?
A: He always gets stuck at 'C'!

Q: Why do zebras have stripes?
A: Because the dots were sold out!

A teacher asks her class: "Let's say I gave you two dogs, two more dogs, and then another two dogs; how many would you have?" Wilma answers: "Seven." Teacher: "No, Wilma, let me repeat the question... If I gave you 2 dogs, 2 more dogs and then another 2, how many would you have in total?" Wilma: "7."

Teacher, getting frustrated now: "Pff, OK...Let's try this another way. If I gave you two oranges, two more oranges, and then another two, how many oranges would you have?" Wilma: "Six."

Teacher: "Exactly! Now, if I gave you two dogs, two more, and another two; how many would you have?" Wilma: "Seven!" Teacher: "Wilma, where on earth do you get seven from?!" Wilma: "Because I already have a dog at home!"

A woman woke up in the morning, next to her husband. She rolled over and told him, "You know what I just dreamed? You would give me a pearl necklace! What do you think that means?" "Tonight, you will know," he replied. That evening, the man came home and gave his wife a small gift-wrapped package. Delighted, his wife opened it, to find a book entitled "Dreams: What Do They Mean?"

Q: How did the eggs leave the highway?
A: They went through the eggs-it.

Q: What did one wall say to the other wall?
A: "I will see you at the corner!"

A policeman stops a woman in a car with a tiger in the front seat. "What are you doing with that tiger?", he asked, "You should take it to the zoo!" The next week, the police officer sees the same woman, with the tiger again in the front seat. This time, both are wearing sunglasses. The policeman pulls the car over. "I thought you were going to take it to the zoo!" The woman replied, "I did. We had such a great time, we are going to the beach this weekend!"

Q: What is a cat's favorite breakfast?
A: Mice Krispies!

Teacher: "Kids, what does the chicken give you?" Student: "Meat!" Teacher: "Very good! Now what does the pig give you?" Student: "Bacon!" Teacher: "Great! And what does the cow give you?" Student: "Homework!"

Q: Why did the ants dance on top of the jam jar?
A: The lid read: 'Twist to open'!

Two flies are eating a turd. One fly says to the other, "I know a hilarious joke, you'll love it!". To which the other fly replies, "It's not a dirty joke, is it? I'm eating…"

Q: What is yellow and laughs at you?
A: A banananana!

A traveler sits down in a restaurant for breakfast. All of a sudden, an elephant walks in, buys a banana ice cream and leaves. The traveler is astounded: "Wow, that's so strange!" The restaurant manager: "Yeah, I agree, up until today he always ordered vanilla ice cream."

Q: Why did the fool sneak quietly past the medicine cabinet?
A: He didn't want to wake up the sleeping pills!

A man arrives at a gas station and asks: "How much for a drop of petrol?" "A drop is free, sir," the gas station clerk says. "Great!", the man replies, "Fill the car up with drops then!"

While mending fences out on the range, a very religious cowboy lost his favorite Bible. He was devastated... However, three weeks later, a bulldog walked up to him, carrying his Bible in its mouth! The cowboy was astonished, he couldn't believe it! He took the precious book out of the bulldog's mouth, thanked him profusely, went on his knees and exclaimed: "It's a miracle!" To which the bulldog replied: "Not really. Your name is written inside the cover..."

Bill and Julie went to the park for a picknick. They brought three cookies. After they both had one, Julie says: "Shall I break the last cookie in two?"
Bill responds, "That's not necessary, I'll eat it like this!"

A man at a wedding says to the waiter, "You know, I used to hate weddings back in the day." "You don't say," the waiter replied, "Why?" The may says, "There would always be an uncle or aunt who'd gave me a push and said, you're up next!". But they stopped once I started doing the same to them at funerals...

Q: Why wasn't the blonde able to add 5 + 10 on her calculator?
A: Because she couldn't figure out where the "10" button was!

Q: What do you call a pig that practices karate?
A: A pork chop!

A cow went to the post office to send a telegram. He took out a blank form and wrote: "Moo. Moo. Moo. Moo. Moo. Moo. Moo. Moo. Moo." When he was done, he gave it to the clerk. The clerk looked at the paper and said to the cow: "There are only 9 words here. We have a special offer: You could send another 'Moo' for the same price." To which the cow replied: "Sorry, but that wouldn't make any sense at all!"

Q: What is fuzzy, green, and if it fell out of a tree it would definitely kill you?
A: A pool table.

Q: What does a cat say when you step on its tail?
A: "Me-OW!"

Q: Why does a seagull fly over the sea?
A: Because if he flew over the bay, he would be called a bagull!

Q: What do you think the difference is between an acoustic guitar and a fish?
A: You can tune a guitar, but you cannot tuna fish!

Q: What did the banana say, when he walked into the doctor's office?
A: "Doctor, I am not peeling well..."

Q: Why didn't the sailors play cards on the boat?
A: Because the captain was on the deck.